BIRDS DO THE STRANGEST THINGS The authors and illustrator of ANIMALS DO THE STRANGEST THINGS have joined forces again to relate the strange and wondrous antics of some lovely birds, both rare and common.

Birds Do The STRANGEST Things

By Leonora and Arthur Hornblow

Illustrations by Michael K. Frith

Step-Up Books   Random House
New York

FOR DEBORAH HORNBLOW

LEONORA & ARTHUR HORNBLOW are the co-authors of four books in the unique Step-Up nature series: *Animals Do the Strangest Things, Birds Do the Strangest Things, Fish Do the Strangest Things,* and *Insects Do the Strangest Things*.

Arthur Hornblow, Jr. is best known as the movie producer who made such famous films as *Oklahoma, Weekend at the Waldorf, Gaslight* and *Witness for the Prosecution*.

Leonora Hornblow is a columnist, novelist, and author of historical books for children.

The Hornblows live in New York City where they are Associate Members of the American Museum of Natural History and the New York Zoological Society.

MICHAEL K. FRITH is from Bermuda and is a Harvard graduate. At Harvard he co-authored the acclaimed parody thriller *Alligator,* majored in Fine Arts, and was president of the *Harvard Lampoon*. He has since illustrated all four of the Hornblows' books and several books for adults.

Mr. Frith, his wife and two daughters live in New York, where he works as an illustrator, designer and editor of children's books.

Contents

The Biggest

On the sandy grasslands of Africa lives the world's biggest bird. It is the ostrich. Some ostriches grow to be eight feet tall. They all have long thin necks. They all have long strong legs. And very strange birds they are. The biggest birds in the world cannot fly.

Zebras and antelopes like to walk along with ostriches. The ostrich is so tall that it is easy for him to watch out for enemies.

When an ostrich sees an enemy, he
runs. This tells the antelopes and
zebras that they should run, too.
Ostriches can run fast. An enemy
might never catch an ostrich if he
did not do a strange thing. Often he
just runs around in big circles. If
he is caught, he fights. He fights
with his feet. He can kill an enemy
with one kick.

The ostrich does not fight his
friends, the zebra and the antelope.
They kick up many small animals
and insects for him. These are
things the ostrich likes to eat.

The female ostrich is not as big as the male. Nor is she as pretty. She is sandy-gray. Her color helps to hide her when she sits on her eggs in the sand. Many ostriches use the same nest. There may be 20 of their huge eggs in one nest. A female sits on the eggs if the day is cold. At night the male sits on the eggs.

There is a story that ostriches bury their heads in the sand to hide from an enemy. Ostriches would never do such a silly thing. They may rest their heads on the sand while they are hatching their eggs. Then it is not easy for them to see an enemy. Maybe they hope an enemy can't see them.

The Flying Jewel

The hummingbird is the only bird that can fly backward. He can fly straight up and down and sideways, too. He can even fly when he is upside down! And perhaps strangest of all, he can fly without going anywhere. He is like a tiny helicopter.

Hummingbirds are the smallest birds in the world. There are many kinds, and they are all beautiful. They are like jewels with wings. Though they are tiny, they are very brave.

A hummingbird seems to know that his enemies cannot catch him. He will fight anything. He can even scare away a hawk.

A hummingbird eats 50 or 60 meals a day. He flashes from flower to flower. He sticks his long bill into a flower and sips the nectar. The sugar in nectar gives the little birds their great strength and energy.

The ruby-throated hummingbird needs all the strength and energy he can get. For every winter this humming-bird makes an amazing flight. First he eats and eats to store up food. He gets quite fat. Then he leaves home. Off he flies for days and days. He flies 500 miles across the ocean to get to a warm place. No one knows how so small a bird can fly so far without food or rest. But the ruby-throat does it every year.

Bigger birds can fly farther. But the ruby-throat is less than three inches long.

Our friend the ostrich is the
biggest bird. He is a good walker
and a great runner. But he cannot
fly at all. It is strange that the
smallest bird flies everywhere.
Even to move an inch he flies. He
cannot walk. He does not have to.
He can get there faster with those
wonderful wings.

Bird About Town

If you live in a city, you have probably seen a pigeon. You may have fed pigeons popcorn in the park. You may have seen them getting under people's feet in the street.

Pigeons have lived with man for at least 5,000 years. Men first used them for food. Then they found out a strange thing. Some pigeons, when taken far away from their nests, flew right back. This gave someone a good idea. Maybe the pigeon could bring a message back with him. Many, many pigeons have been trained to do this.

They are called homing pigeons. A homing pigeon carries the message in a little tube. The tube is put on the bird's leg.

Before radio, the homing pigeon's most important use was in war time. Pigeons will fly right through smoke and gun fire. They will fly anywhere. Some pigeons have been given medals for bravery by the army. Pigeons don't care about medals. All they want is to get home.

The Flying Submarine

The loon is the best swimmer of
all the birds. He can swim the
fastest. He can dive the deepest.
He can stay under water longer
than any other bird. His legs are
set far back on his body. They
help him when he is swimming.

The loon is a fine flier, too. He can fly a mile a minute. But he has trouble getting up in the air. He cannot take off from land. He has to run along on top of the water. Sometimes he runs for a quarter of a mile to get up enough speed to take off.

He also has a hard time landing. He cannot come down on the water softly. He lands with a great big splash. Loons like to be in the water best. They can hardly stand up on land.

But the loons have to come out
of the water to lay their eggs. They
make a nest for their eggs on land.

After the eggs are hatched, the
baby loons go into the water. Their
parents take them. They want to
teach the babies to swim. At first,
little loons ride around on the
grownups' backs. Then the parents
slowly sink under the water. Only
their heads show. But the babies know
that their parents are below them.

Soon the little loons learn to swim alone.

One of the strangest things about the loon is his cry. It may sound like a terrible scream for help. Or a ghost laughing on Halloween. It is a very scary sound. The cry has given the loon his name. Loon is short for lunatic. The word lunatic means crazy. There is an old saying, "crazy as a loon." But the only thing crazy about the loon is the noise he makes.

King of the Air

The American bald eagle is the mighty hunter of the sky. Men have always admired him.

Few birds can fly as high as the eagle. He circles in the air looking for food. He can see a rabbit on the ground when he is a mile up in the air. He can see a fish from up there, too. Down he dives to get his food. He rarely misses.

But the mighty eagle is also a thief. He often steals his food from another bird. He waits until the other bird catches a fish. Then he dives straight at him. The other bird is often frightened by the eagle. So he drops his fish. The eagle will catch the fish before it hits the ground. Then back he flies to his huge high nest to enjoy his stolen supper.

The Odd One

There are many birds that cannot fly. But the kiwi is the only bird that doesn't have wings. His feathers are strange, too. They look like hair. Hidden under the hairy feathers are two small knobs. Maybe these knobs were wings long ago.

Kiwis live under ground at the bottom of trees. They dig holes to live in. The female kiwi lays her eggs there. A kiwi is only as big as a chicken. But each egg weighs a whole pound.

A kiwi does not leave his underground home until night comes. Then he goes out hunting for his favorite food— worms. His long bill is a marvelous tool for worm hunting. The kiwi moves around in the dark, smelling the ground. He can smell a worm down below. He stamps with his big feet. The worm comes up to see what is happening. Good-by worm!

Kiwis are found only in New Zealand. They may not be beautiful birds but they surely are strange.

The Singing Marvel

Do you want to hear the songs of many birds? Then go find a mockingbird. He can sing his own beautiful song. He can also sing the song of almost any bird he hears. He can copy other sounds. He can even copy the bark of a dog or a policeman's whistle.

He often sings all the songs and sounds he knows, one right after the other. Maybe this is his way of saying, "Listen to the mockingbird."

The Marvelous Mimic

Mockingbirds copy sounds and other birds' songs. Mynah birds copy people's words.

The common mynah lives in India. Until he meets people, he just laughs and whistles and makes crazy sounds. But he can be taught to talk. He can learn to talk better than any other bird, even a parrot. If you are looking for a bird that will answer you, visit a pet shop and say hello to a mynah.

21

Rubber Neck

Flamingos look beautiful when they
fly. On the ground you have to see
them to believe them. A flamingo
bends his long neck like a hose.
His long legs are like sticks. His
beak looks like a scoop. He uses it
to eat upside down!

He puts his head into the water
upside down. He takes a big
mouthful of mud. He hopes
to find shrimps and snails
in it. He swallows some
mud. He likes the mud, too.

Flamingos even build their nests of mud. Their nests look like big mud pies. While the flamingos are sitting on their eggs, they like everything to be quiet.

Airplanes bother them. They will leave their nests if too many airplanes fly over them. Flamingos are nervous birds. Noisy people bother them, too. Please leave them alone.

The Lone Bandit

No one likes a shrike—
probably not even other
shrikes. He is a small bird
with a hooked beak. He has
a band of black feathers around
his eyes. This makes him look
like a bandit. He acts like a
bandit, too. He sits and waits
for a mouse, a frog, a snake
or another bird to pass by.
Almost anything looks fine to
him. Even another shrike. He
hits it with his sharp beak. It
falls to the ground. Then the
shrike does a very strange thing.

He picks it up with his beak. He flies with it to a thorny bush. If there is no bush, he may take it to a barbed-wire fence. He always hangs up his prey, the way a butcher hangs up his meat. This is why he is sometimes called the butcher bird.

The butcher bird often eats what he has hung up, right away. But if there is more to capture, he does not always stop to eat. He flies away to look for more. Maybe he wants to be sure that there is always food in his butcher shop.

The Builder

Can you believe that a bird can build a house? Well, there is one that does. When explorers in New Guinea first saw these houses, they thought children had built them. But bowerbirds had built them. What wonderful bowers they are! Many have roofs. Some even have rooms. There are different kinds of bowerbirds. They build different kinds of bowers.

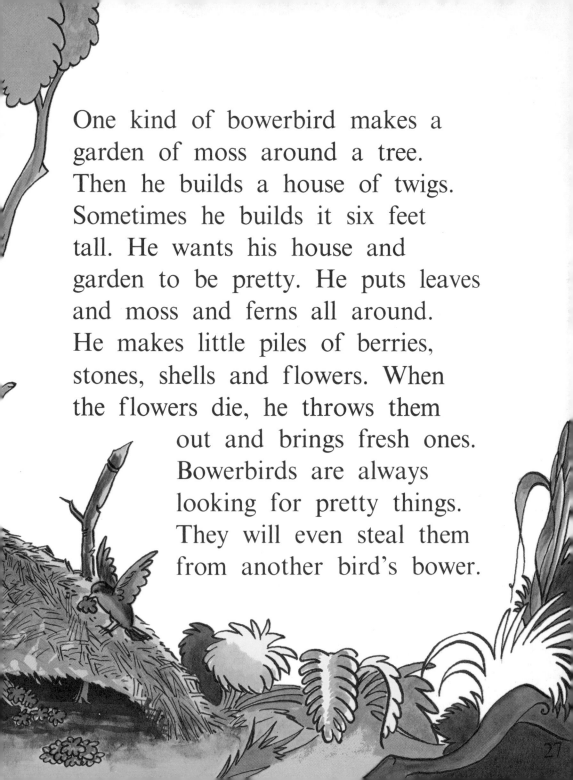

One kind of bowerbird makes a
garden of moss around a tree.
Then he builds a house of twigs.
Sometimes he builds it six feet
tall. He wants his house and
garden to be pretty. He puts leaves
and moss and ferns all around.
He makes little piles of berries,
stones, shells and flowers. When
the flowers die, he throws them
out and brings fresh ones.
Bowerbirds are always
looking for pretty things.
They will even steal them
from another bird's bower.

The blue satin bowerbird starts his bower with a mat of twigs. In the middle of the mat he builds two walls of twigs. The blue satin bowerbird wants his bower to be pretty. His idea of something pretty is something blue. He finds blue flowers and feathers, shells and berries. Everything he puts in his house is blue.

Most amazing of all, the blue satin bowerbird can paint the inside of his bower blue. He makes his paint out of charcoal and berry juice. He even makes a paint brush out of a piece of bark. He holds the brush in his beak.

It may take a bowerbird months to build his bower. He would like to share it with a lady bowerbird. When one comes along, the male stops work on the house. He does a dance for her. After a while she goes in to see if she likes the bower.

But she never uses the bower for a nest. When the time comes to lay her eggs she flies away. She makes a plain nest for herself and her children. Her husband, the wonderful builder, does not help her. He does not even know he has children. All he cares about is looking after his bower.

The Silent Hunter

Some owls look wise.
Some owls look gentle.
But don't be fooled by looks.
No owl is wise. Nor are any
owls gentle.

There are many kinds of owls.
Some are as small as sparrows.
Others are as big as roosters.
Large or small, all owls have
sharp curved claws and strong
hooked beaks. And by nature
all owls are great hunters.

The night owl goes out hunting as soon as it is dark. He kills and eats things that walk or fly, crawl or swim. Owls can see the smallest creatures. Owls can hear the smallest creatures. They can see and hear them day or night.

Owls use both their eyes and ears when they hunt in the dark, dark night. They see and hear a beetle crawling by. Owls eat a lot of beetles. An owl does not miss a thing. Not even a quiet little mouse.

An owl will kill and eat a skunk.
This could be why owls' feathers
sometimes have an awful smell.
The wing feathers of night owls
are very soft. They can fly right
past you without making a sound.

There is another strange thing about
their feathers. They can puff them
all up. Then owls look twice as big
as they really are. They do this to
show off to their mates. Or to scare
enemies away from their nests.

An owl looks strange when he is all puffed up. He also looks strange when he is watching something move. He follows it with his eyes. But his eyes can only see straight ahead. So he has to move his whole head. His head seems to turn all the way around and upside down. Sometimes it looks as if he is going to twist it right off!

Owls make all kinds of sounds. But their best-known sound is "hoo-hoo." And who-who wants to be an owl?

The Honey Scout

A little bird called the honey guide lives in Africa. He is always on the lookout for animals or men who want honey. Men in Africa know this. So when they want honey, they look for a honey guide. He always leads them to the nests of honeybees.

The honey guide starts chirping as soon as he sees a hunter. Then off he flies. The hunter follows as fast as he can. If he is slow, the bird waits and chirps even louder.

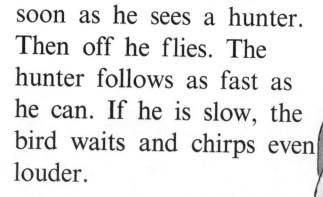

A honey guide is a very good guide. He flies and chirps to keep a hunter going the right way. When at last they get to the honey, the guide waits. He sits on the tree. He cannot get to the comb by himself. That is why he brings men and animals to honey. The strange thing is that he wants the wax in the honeycomb. Men and animals don't want the wax. They want the honey. So both the hunters and the honey guides are happy.

The Beach Cleaner

Herring gulls are called "sea" gulls. Yet they live near lakes and rivers, too. They rarely go far out to sea. Sometimes gulls will follow a ship for miles. Not because they like the sea, or the ship. What they like is the leftover food that people throw overboard. Gulls are great garbage collectors.

Most of the time gulls stay around docks and beaches looking for food. When a gull finds something, he eats it. He is always eating.

A gull will eat almost anything. If a dead fish washes up on the beach, it does not stay there long. The minute a gull sees it he goes for it. When other gulls see one gull go for something, they go too. Then they usually fight over every scrap. Soon there is nothing left. That is why gulls are such good friends to man. They help to keep our beaches clean.

Sometimes a gull will find shellfish
near the sea. Gulls love shellfish.
But a gull cannot open a shellfish
with his beak. So he flies with it
high up in the air. When he is over
some rocks, or a hard road, or even
a car, he drops the shellfish. It
smashes open. The gull dives down
after it. He knows that if he does not
get there fast, another gull will be
eating his shellfish.

There is a strange thing about
herring gulls and food. There is
one time in their lives when they
are fussy about eating. That is
when they are babies.

As soon as a baby gull is hatched, he looks for something red. Every grown-up gull has a red spot on its beak. The baby pecks at his parent's red spot. His parents won't feed him unless he does. Stranger still, the baby will not eat unless he finds something red to peck. He will just starve.

You can try to feed a baby gull. But first you must show him something red. Almost any red thing will do.

By the time the baby leaves the nest he is no longer fussy about pecking something red, or about his food. Off he flies to help keep the beaches clean.

The Fooler

The European cuckoo is one of the birds whose call is its own name. When you hear, "Cuckoo, cuckoo," you know who it is. But a cuckoo can change its call and the way it flies. It can fool you.

Strangest of all is the way it can fool other birds. A female cuckoo puts her eggs in some other bird's nest. She picks the nest of a bird whose eggs are the same color as her eggs. Then she flies away forever. The other poor bird hatches the cuckoo eggs.

When the baby cuckoo hatches, it
is almost always bigger than the
other babies in the nest. It may
even grow bigger than the bird who
hatched it. But she still thinks it
is her own child. She keeps on
feeding it.

As soon as the little cuckoo learns
to fly, it leaves the nest. It goes
to meet other cuckoos. They may
be hundreds of miles away. But
the young cuckoo finds them. This
is one of the strange things that
happens in the world of birds.

The Oily Bird

The oilbird loves the dark.
He makes his nest inside the
darkest cave he can find. Bats
live in these same caves with
him. Hundreds of oilbirds and
bats fly around together in
the blackest caves. They never
hit anything.

Like the bat, an oilbird can
send out signals as he flies.
The signal is a ticking sound.

The ticking sound hits whatever is in front of him, and echoes back. The echo tells the oilbird something is ahead.

As soon as the sun goes down, the oilbirds all fly out of their caves and into the dark forests. There they eat fruit and nuts from palm trees. These nuts are very oily. Because he eats nuts all the time, he gets oily, too. This is why he is called the oilbird.

The oilbird will fly for miles looking for food. Sometimes he flies as far as fifty miles. But he is sure to be home again before the sun comes out.

The Show-Off

To win a lady peahen's love the peacock does a strange and wonderful thing. He opens his tail feathers like a great big fan. It is the most remarkable sight in the world of birds.

The peacock seems to know it. He poses for the peahen. He parades like a soldier. And to finish the show, he does a little dance.

The peahen makes believe she does not see him. For a long time she looks the other way. But after a while she is won by so much beauty.

The peacock is a member of the chicken family. He is prettier. But his little cousin, the chicken, is much more useful. In fact, the chicken is perhaps the most useful bird on earth.

Never tell that to a peacock!

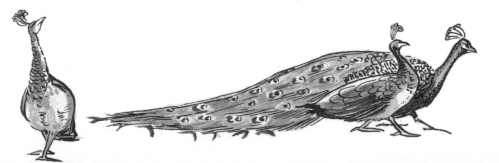

Daddy-Longlegs

High on the roofs of many houses in Europe there are huge nests. They are the nests of the beautiful white storks. The same storks may return to the same nests year after year. They are wonderful to watch as they come and go.

One stork stays in the nest to watch over the baby storks. The other goes off looking for food. The stork in the nest watches the sky, waiting for the other one to come home. When they meet again, they do a strange and wonderful thing. The stork in the nest stands up and rattles its beak. The other stork rattles its beak in answer. They bow to each other. They twist their necks back and around and about. This is their way of talking. For they have no voices at all.

47

The storks live in their roof
nests all through the summer.
But when the cold days begin,
they meet out in the fields. There
they stand. They rattle their bills
for a long time.

Then suddenly they rise high in
the air. They are off on one of
the greatest trips in the world of
birds. The young storks leave first.
They have never taken this trip
before. There is no one to show
them the way. But they
know just where they are
going. They are going to
Africa, 6,000 miles away.

The people are sad
to see them go.
They love to have the storks
living up on their roofs.
They believe that it is good
luck to have a stork on their house.

Some people put big baskets and
wagon wheels on their roofs. They
hope the storks will build nests in
them when they come back. If they
do, the people are very happy. It
is fun to have another family on
the roof.

The Hide-Away Bird

There are many kinds of birds' nests. But the strangest of all is the hornbill's.

Two hornbills find a tree with a hole in it. The female climbs in. Then they plaster the front of the hole. They make the plaster out of mud. It is very strong. They leave a little opening. It is just big enough to let the male feed the female. He feeds her while she sits on her eggs. Nothing can get at her or her eggs in her sealed-up nest.

The little hornbills are hatched in the hole. The father feeds his sealed-up family. His tail gets worn from rubbing against the tree. He gets tired and thin. After two or three months the mother breaks out. She is fat and has grown a new set of feathers. She is stiff from sitting in such a small place. But she takes over the feeding of the babies.

It is hard to believe that sometimes the babies plaster themselves back into the hole. Not the mother. She is glad to be out.

All Dressed Up

The penguin looks funny and friendly. His feathers are black and white. So it seems as if he is wearing a neat little suit and a white shirt. He stands up straight on his short legs. He looks like a little person all dressed up.

Not all penguins are little. The biggest is the emperor penguin. He may grow to be four feet tall.

The emperor penguin lives near the South Pole, far, far away from people. It is always cold there. In his whole life the emperor never touches dry land! He is always on the ice and snow, or in the cold water.

It is a wonderful sight to see penguins marching across the ice. They usually waddle along in a line, one by one. Sometimes they drop down on their stomachs and push themselves along with their feet and wings. They can go quite fast. They zip along on the ice and snow like sleds. It must be fun.

There is a long, dark night near the South Pole. The sun does not shine for half the year. This is when the mother penguin lays her egg. Emperor penguins do not have nests. As soon as the egg is laid, the father puts it on his feet. He holds it to keep it from freezing on the ice. He does not leave the egg for a moment. The father's warm feathers cover the egg like a blanket. For two months he holds it.

The coldest winds on earth blow around him. But he hardly moves. And he does not eat. When the little penguin is hatched, the mother takes over. Now she will help to look after the baby. At last the hungry father can get something to eat. Soon the little penguin can waddle about. Then all the parents gather all the children together in a big "kindergarten." The big penguins stand around the little ones. They make a fence of grown-up penguins. This helps to keep some of the snow and wind away from the young ones.

The little penguins will never learn to fly. Penguins' wings are too small. But penguins are wonderful swimmers. And their wings help them in the water. They love the cold, rough sea. They play in the waves. They dive for food. But they don't stay under very long. They have to come up for air.

The penguin has a strange way of getting out of the water. He dives down under the water. Then he swims toward the shore as fast as he can. Just before he reaches the land, he jumps out.

He may jump six feet in the air.
But he always lands on his feet.
He goes back in the water when he
gets hungry. He does not know how
to eat on land. This can make life
hard for a penguin if he is taken
to a zoo. He has to be taught to
eat the fish that are thrown to
him or given to him. Sometimes
this takes weeks. But he always
learns. And he eats them
like a little man.

Hammer-Head

If you watch a woodpecker in the
woods, you will see him
slowly hopping up the
side of a tree. He stops.
He puts his head to one
side. He listens. He is
listening for the sounds
of insects inside the tree.
If he hears any, he leans
back on his stiff tail. Then,
"rat-a-tat-tat." He pounds
with his sharp beak. He
makes a small hole in the
tree. Into the hole goes his
long, sticky tongue. Out come
the insects.

No other bird can use his head as a hammer. No other bird has such a hard head.

The woodpecker doesn't hammer just to get insects. It is also one of his ways of talking. He has a voice. But usually he hammers on roofs or dead logs to let other woodpeckers know he is there. His hammering will let you know he is there, too. Go have a look at him. He may be hammering a big hole in a tree. When it is big enough, he and a lady woodpecker will probably use it as a nest. They will line the nest with chips of wood. And in it they will raise more little hammer-heads.

Bye-Bye Birdie

The world is full of birds. Some of them are around all the time. Others, like the swallow, come and go.

Male birds are usually prettier than females. And they usually sing the most. We love to listen to them. But they are not singing for us. They are talking to other birds. A male goldfinch might sing to a lady goldfinch, "Look at me. I am pretty." If she agrees, she makes a nest while he sings. But most bird songs are fighting songs. Many birds, like robins and orioles, take certain trees for themselves.

A robin's song may really be a call to a blue jay, "Keep out! This is my tree."

A bird with a very loud call is the crow. Not all people like crows. They put up scarecrows to keep crows away from seeds. But scarecrows don't always scare crows. They sit right on them and say, "Caw-caw-caw." They seem to be laughing. Could they be laughing at us? After all, people are strange and wonderful, too.

The
STEP-UP Books

NATURE LIBRARY

ANIMALS DO THE STRANGEST THINGS

BIRDS DO THE STRANGEST THINGS

FISH DO THE STRANGEST THINGS

INSECTS DO THE STRANGEST THINGS

Story of AMERICA

Meet THE NORTH AMERICAN INDIANS   THE ADVENTURES OF LEWIS AND CLARK

Meet THE MEN WHO SAILED THE SEAS   Meet ANDREW JACKSON

Meet CHRISTOPHER COLUMBUS   Meet ABRAHAM LINCOLN

Meet THE PILGRIM FATHERS   Meet ROBERT E. LEE

Meet BENJAMIN FRANKLIN   Meet THEODORE ROOSEVELT

Meet GEORGE WASHINGTON   Meet JOHN F. KENNEDY

Meet THOMAS JEFFERSON   Meet MARTIN LUTHER KING, JR.

THE STORY OF FLIGHT